IT'S MY STATE!

NORTH DAKOTA

Doug Sanders

Cavendish
Square

New York

Published in 2014 by Cavendish Square Publishing, LLC
303 Park Avenue South, Suite 1247, New York, NY 10010

Library of Congress Cataloging-in-Publication Data

Sanders, Doug, 1972-
 North Dakota / Doug Sanders.
   pages cm. — (It's my state)
 Includes index.
 ISBN 978-1-62712-223-8 (hardcover) ISBN 978-1-62712-483-6 (paperback) ISBN 978-1-62712-234-4 (ebook)
 1. North Dakota—Juvenile literature. I. Title.

 F636.3.S36 2014b
 978.4—dc23

                    2013034181

This edition developed for Cavendish Square Publishing by RJF Publishing LLC (www.RJFpublishing.com)
Series Designer, Second Edition: Tammy West/Westgraphix LLC
Editorial Director: Dean Miller
Editor: Sara Howell
Copy Editor: Cynthia Roby
Art Director: Jeffrey Talbot
Layout Design: Erica Clendening
Production Manager: Jennifer Ryder-Talbot

CONTENTS

State Flower: Wild Prairie Rose

This flower has five bright pink petals arranged around a yellow center. Wild prairie roses are usually found in pastures, meadows, and beside the state's roads. They are most common in the moist and cool soils of eastern and central North Dakota.

State Bird: Western Meadowlark

Meadowlarks eat mostly spiders and insects in the summer and seeds in the winter. President Theodore Roosevelt once described the state bird as "one of our sweetest, loudest songsters. . . . The Plains air seems to give it voice and it will perch on top of a bush or tree and sing for hours in rich, bubbling tones."

State Insect: Convergent Lady Beetle

Convergent lady beetles, commonly called ladybugs, became the state insect in 2011 when a group of students from Kenmare Elementary School suggested the idea to an official from the state house of representatives. The convergent lady beetle's main food is a type of insect called an aphid.

State Beverage: Milk

North Dakota's legislature chose milk as the official state beverage to highlight the importance of the dairy industry. Out of North Dakota's 1.79 million cows, about 30,000 are raised for milk and produce enough milk each year to fill 1 billion glasses!

State Fruit: Chokecherry

The chokecherry, commonly found throughout the state, was made the state fruit in 2007. The red and black fruit of the chokecherry plant has a sour, bitter taste. It was one of the most important fruits in many Native American diets for many years, and the bark of the plant was used as a medicine.

State Dance: Square Dance

North Dakota's square dancers have held an annual convention for more than 50 years, usually in April. Following the instructions of the caller, groups of couples, typically four, move in rhythmic patterns, all to the sounds of a fiddle, accordion, banjo, or guitar.

NORTH DAKOTA

CANADA

Fortuna

Fort Union
Trading Post
National
Historic
Site

Williston

Missouri River

Theodore Roosevelt
National Park
North Unit

Theodore Roosevelt
National Park
South Unit

Little Missouri River

White Butte

Dickinson

Dakota
Dinosaur
Museum

Cedar River
National Grassland

North
Lemmon

Turtle Mountains

Bottineau

Minot

Mouse River

Rugby

International
Peace
Garden

GEOGRAPHIC CENTER
OF NORTH AMERICA

Neche

Pembina River

Pembina Mountains

Grafton

Red River

Devils
Lake

Devils Lake

Grand
Forks

Sheyenne River

Lake
Sakakawea

Garrison Dam

Fort
Mandan
Historical
Site

Mandan

Lake Oahe

Bismarck

James River

Jamestown

Frontier Village

Forbes

Sheyenne
State Forest

Sheyenne National Grassland

Sunflowers

Fargo

Wahpeton

Bois de Sioux River

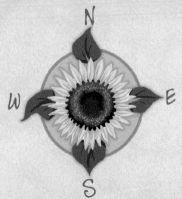

N
W   E
S

The Peace Garden State

About 70 million years ago, the area that includes present-day North Dakota was almost entirely covered by a shallow, warm sea. By 65 million years ago, the water had begun draining from the western parts of the state. A coastal plain formed in its place. The plain was made up of woodlands, marshes, and small ponds. Snails, clams, insects, fish, and amphibians clustered in the damp swampland. Predators much like today's crocodiles, reaching over 12 feet (3.6 m) long, drifted through the waters. The state was clearly a much different place then.

By 30 million years ago, North Dakota started to look similar to how it appears today. The vast bodies of water continued to shrink as more land was added to the plains. Eventually North Dakota's four main land regions began to emerge. Many types of animals and plants thrived in the different landscapes.

The Red River Valley

The Red River forms the state's eastern border, separating North Dakota from Minnesota. The Red River valley runs along each side of this important waterway. In North Dakota the Red River valley is a thin strip of land that stretches along the entire eastern portion

Quick Facts

North Dakota's Borders

North	Canada
South	South Dakota
East	Minnesota
West	Montana

of the state. Flat and fertile, the valley was once part of the floor of the ancient Lake Agassiz. The lake formed at the end of the last Ice Age about 10,000 years ago. When the water eventually drained away, it exposed a layer of earth rich in nutrients and deposits. This part of the state is one of the most fertile areas in the world. It is not surprising, then, that the Red River valley is one of North Dakota's main agricultural regions. Wheat is one of the most important crops grown in this region. Flax, barley, sugar beets, and sunflowers also thrive there.

The Red River valley is home to the lowest elevation in the state. The land near Pembina, in North Dakota's northeastern corner, is only around 750 feet (229 m) above sea level. Fargo, the state's largest city, is found in this region, along with Grand Forks, another major city. Smaller towns can also be found spread throughout the region. Most North Dakotans live in this part of the state.

What was once the floor of Lake Agassiz is now the fertile Red River valley. Deposits from the ancient body of water have made the region's soil some of the richest in the country.

This snow-covered prairie is near the town of Rolla, in the north-central part of the state.

Drift Prairie

Heading west from the Red River valley, the landscape starts to display a little more variety. Occasionally a hill gently lifts from the otherwise flat land. Here and there, a small butte, or steep outcropping, pokes out of the plains. This region is called North Dakota's drift prairie, an area where the land rises gradually from 200 feet (61 m) to 2,000 feet (610 m). In general, the drift prairie gains elevation along its western and southwestern edges. In the north, though, near the Pembina Hills and the Turtle Mountains, the sloping land is among the steepest in the state. Some of these uplands are covered in the state's largest forests.

The drift prairie is known for its rich soil. Glaciers, or slow-moving masses of ice, are responsible for making the region so fertile. During the last Ice

Age, glaciers slowly receded, moving north across the land. As they shrank and shifted, they left behind deposits of soil, minerals, and other materials that help plants thrive. Drift is the name given to this rich mixture.

Those who think the plains are nothing more than flat grasslands could not be more wrong. To the west, gently rolling hills mark the horizon. Streams run at the base of shallow valleys and many lakes dot the land. Several lakes lie in the pockets carved out by glaciers. These small bodies of water are called prairie potholes. Ducks and geese often stop there during their annual migrations.

The geographic center of North America is located in the drift prairie. It is found near the town of Rugby in the north-central portion of the state. A 15-foot-(4.5 m) tall rock monument marks the place. Some claim that the true center of the continent is a short distance away on private property in a farmer's field. Either way you look at it, this part of the state is approximately 1,500 miles (2,414 km) from the Atlantic, Pacific, and Arctic oceans and the Gulf of Mexico.

This monument, built in 1931, claims Rugby as the geological center of North America. Near the monument are the flags of North America's largest three countries—the United States, Mexico, and Canada.

The Little Missouri National Grassland in southwestern North Dakota is ideal for ranching. Cattle feed on the rich supply of grass.

The Great Plains

The Great Plains make up almost all of southwestern North Dakota. The plains are a part of the vast plateau that runs from northern Canada to southern Texas. The portion that includes North Dakota is called the Missouri Plateau. The region begins at Couteau Slope, near the eastern bank of the Missouri River. The slope is about 300 to 400 feet (91–122 m) tall and marks a dividing point between the drift prairie and the Great Plains beyond. Cattle graze the Great Plains's hills and grasslands. The area is also known for its mineral deposits, oil, and coal.

The Missouri Plateau contains the highest elevations in the state. They range from 2,000 feet (610 m) to more than 3,000 feet (914 m). North Dakota's highest point, White Butte, is found in the southwestern part of the state. White Butte is 3,506 feet (1,068 m).

Quick Facts

North Dakota's nickname, the Peace Garden State, comes from the International Peace Garden, a botanical garden on the state's northern border with Canada. The garden is a symbol of friendship between Canada and the United States.

Lake Sakakawea is named for the Shoshone/Hidatsa woman who acted as a guide and interpreter for Lewis and Clark on their expedition. She is often called Sacagawea, but Native Americans in North Dakota believe her name was actually Sakakawea.

The state's lifeline, the Missouri River, runs through the Great Plains. When the Garrison Dam was built across the Missouri River starting in the late 1940s, Lake Sakakawea was formed. The lake stretches nearly 200 miles (322 km) to the west and has 1,340 miles (2,156 km) of shoreline. That is more shoreline than the entire coast of California. Many residents and visitors enjoy boating and fishing in the lake's blue waters.

The Missouri River Breaks region includes the land on both sides of the Missouri River. Trees line the riverbanks in tight clusters. To the south and west of the river is a part of the plains called the Slope. This area is known for its many hills, valleys, and buttes.

The Badlands

Located in the western part of the state, the badlands are a thin valley made up mostly of sandstone, shale, and clay. The valley is about 190 miles (305 km) long and around 6 to 20 miles (9.6–32 km) wide. The Lakota (groups of Native Americans who live in the region) call the badlands "Mako Shika," or "where the land breaks." Many first-time visitors are not ready for the shock and surprise that await them when they reach this part of North Dakota. After seeing vast stretches of gently rolling grasslands, visitors may feel as though they have suddenly entered another planet. Towering buttes, striped with layers of brown and red, twist and fold as far as the eye can see. Cone-shaped mounds and rounded domes poke up in the most unexpected places. The unusual formations of the badlands offer some of the state's most memorable scenery.

The strange shapes found in the badlands were created over millions of years. When western North Dakota was part of an inland sea 70 million years ago,

Theodore Roosevelt National Park was created in 1947 to protect the badlands and the plants and animals that live there.

layer upon layer of sediment—dirt, rock, minerals, and other natural materials—collected on the sea floor. After the water drained away, the buttes of the badlands were exposed. Their striking bands of color are the traces of each of the deposited layers. Millions of years of wind and water then sculpted the structures into the shapes seen today.

Before he became US president, Theodore Roosevelt came to the area in 1883 to start a ranching operation. Struck by the area's rugged beauty, Roosevelt always held a special place in his heart for the badlands. In 1947, Theodore Roosevelt National Park was created to protect this rare and strange stretch of the state. It is the only national park in North Dakota. Roosevelt perhaps best summed up the beauty of the entire region when he said, "The Badlands . . . are so fantastically broken in form and so bizarre in color as to seem hardly properly to belong to this earth."

Climate

North Dakota has what is called a continental climate. That means hot summers and cold winters, little humidity, and small amounts of rain. It also means extremes in temperatures. The climate is the result of North Dakota's location. On the flat plains in the center of the United States there are few natural barriers such as tall mountains. The winds move freely across the grasslands. Icy blasts can cause the temperature to fall rapidly over the course of a few hours.

The average summer temperature in the northern part of the state is about 65°F (18.3°C). North Dakotans living in the southern sections of the state have slightly warmer summers with average temperatures of about 70°F (21°C).

North Dakota's winters can be brutal. Fierce blasts of wind and ice often come racing in from all directions.

Winter temperatures average about 2°F (-16.6°C) in some parts of the state. The northeastern portion of the state tends to be colder than the southern and southwestern parts.

The amount of precipitation—rain, snow, sleet, and hail—that falls in North Dakota changes as you move across the state. North Dakota's average snowfall is about 30 inches (76 cm) per year. The east usually receives more rain than the west. An average of 22 inches (56 cm) of rain falls each year in the Red River valley. Western North Dakota is drier, with parts of the region receiving less than 15 inches (38 cm) of rain per year. The most rain usually falls on North Dakota from early spring through late summer.

The population of bison—a symbol of the plains—has been steadily climbing in North Dakota in the past few decades.

Summer is the ideal time to enjoy North Dakota. The amount of sunlight the state receives then is a powerful reminder of how far north it is. From mid-May through July, the state is blessed with more than fifteen hours of sunlight each day.

Wild North Dakota

North Dakota has a variety of plant and animal life. The plains are mostly treeless, so only about 1 percent of the state is covered in forest. Trees that grow in the eastern part of the state include poplar, oak, and aspen. Juniper is found on some of the state's hillsides. Cottonwood, ash, and elm trees huddle along the Missouri River Breaks. From a distance you might be able to trace the river's flow by following the rows of trees clustered on the riverbanks.

North Dakotans are treated to large areas of wild grasses and flowers that thrive on the plains. Pasqueflowers, prairie mallows, black-eyed Susans, and wild prairie roses add dots of color to the green and golden grass. Together these plants provide much-needed cover and food for many of North Dakota's birds and mammals.

When driving through Theodore Roosevelt National Park it is possible to see many different types of animals. These include mule deer, white-tailed deer, prairie dogs, pronghorn antelope, bison, bighorn sheep, wild turkeys, and bull snakes. Most of these animals can be found in other parts of the state, too. Patches of prairie grass often hide birds such as ring-necked pheasants, sharp-tailed grouse, and gray partridge. The prairie is also home to white-tailed jackrabbits and ground squirrels.

If you walk or hike along one of the state's many trails you might hear a chorus of barks and yelps. These sounds are probably coming from prairie dogs. Large colonies of black-tailed prairie dogs are spread across North Dakota. They live in a complex maze of tunnels and dens hidden beneath the prairie.

By keeping a watchful eye, prairie dogs can pop back into their dens at the first sign of danger.

Prairie dog towns are important to the survival of other types of animals, too. Badgers, coyotes, and long-tailed weasels live around the prairie dog towns, using the small animals as food. Burrowing owls, prairie rattlesnakes, cottontail rabbits, and the endangered black-footed ferret often use abandoned prairie dog tunnels and dens. These animals use the underground system to hide from predators or to bear and raise their young.

Water may be precious on the plains, but fishing is still a major pastime in North Dakota. Fishers can enjoy their sport all year—from a boat or from the shore of lakes and ponds. They can even fish by drilling holes through thick layers of ice. Devils Lake, the state's largest natural body of water, is known to some people as the "Perch Capital of the World." Colorful perch thrive in the lake, along with a healthy supply of walleye, northern pike, and white bass.

Endangered Wildlife

North Dakotans work together to try to protect their wildlife. Many laws ban the hunting of animals with small populations. Concerned citizens and government officials have also established laws and programs that protect portions of land and the plants and animals living there.

The state's bighorn sheep are one endangered animal population that is making a comeback. The bighorn sheep was once a common sight along the Missouri and Little Missouri rivers. By the late 1800s, though, human settlement and the increased hunting in the area reduced the population. The sheep almost completely disappeared from this part of the plains. In 1905, North Dakota's last bighorn sheep was killed near Magpie Creek, in southern McKenzie County. It was not until

1956 that efforts were made to restore the bighorn sheep population. Eighteen bighorn sheep were brought from Canada to the North Dakota badlands. They now live in nine areas in the badlands and along the Little Missouri River. In 2013, their population had reached about 300 animals and continues to grow. This is just one of the state's success stories.

For many years people thought that black bears and mountain lions no longer lived in the state. However, since 1990, state residents have reported seeing several mountain lions each year. Black bears have also been spotted, though it is difficult to determine how many bears live in the state. These sightings are strong signs that the state's efforts to protect its native species are working.

Thanks to conservation efforts, the bighorn sheep has slowly become a more common sight on the plains of western North Dakota.

Richardson's Ground Squirrel

North Dakota gets one of its nicknames, the Flickertail State, from these hardworking rodents. They flick their tails while running across the prairie or just before escaping down a hole. These squirrels have short ears and fuzzy tails tinged with black. They are found throughout the northern and eastern portions of the state.

Snow Goose

In flight, snow geese can reach speeds of up to 40 miles per hour (64 km/h). When migrating, they can travel long distances—sometimes up to 1,500 miles (2,414 km) nonstop. The town of Kenmare is considered the goose capital of North Dakota. Nearly 400,000 birds nest in the area. As many as 2 million snow geese may pass through the state each year.

Western Painted Turtle

This turtle is known for the yellow stripes and patterns on its face, neck, and undersides. It eats mostly minnows, insects, and worms. To honor this animal, Turtle Lake has built a turtle sculpture that weighs 2 tons (1.8 t). The town is also the home of the annual Turtle Days festival and the USA and World Championship Turtle Races.

Ring-Necked Pheasant

These birds are originally from Asia and were probably first introduced to the state in the early 1900s. Over the years, the ring-necked pheasant has adapted well to the Great Plains. Pheasant populations are small in other parts of the country, but in North Dakota their numbers have increased since the 1960s.

Bison

Bison (often called buffalo) feast on the wheatgrass, buffalo grass, and blue grama that grow on the plains. Bison are one of the largest mammals in North America. Adult males can weigh more than 2,000 pounds (907 kg) and stand more than 6 feet (1.8 m) tall. They can live to be around thirty years old.

Black-Eyed Susan

In July, the yellow daisy-like blooms of the black-eyed Susan are a common sight on North Dakota's prairies. The plant grows well at the bases of hills, the bottoms of valleys, and the moister parts of the grasslands. The flower can thrive mostly anywhere in the state. Black-eyed Susans can grow up to 2 feet (0.6 m) tall.

From the Beginning

Humans first entered North Dakota about 12,000 years ago, around the end of the last Ice Age. These people were known as the Paleo-Indians. Most came to North America across the land bridge that once connected present-day Alaska and Siberia. Eventually they spread across the continent, working their way south. On the plains, the Paleo-Indians hunted mammoths, mastodons, and other large mammals. The area was good for hunting and gathering foods such as nuts, berries, and plants.

From 5500 to 400 BC, the Paleo-Indians broke into small, wandering bands. They followed the bison and sought shelter in the warm, dry grasslands. The years between 400 BC and AD 1000 brought another shift in their lifestyle. They continued to hunt and gather but began settling into more permanent villages and communities. The Paleo-Indians produced pottery and built elaborate burial mounds to honor their dead. Some of these mounds still exist and are found across the Midwest. From AD 1000 on, villages grew larger and more complex. North Dakota's native residents built large lodges out of earth. They also began growing corn, beans, squash, sunflowers, and tobacco in nearby fields.

In this photograph from the 1890s, a Lakota child stands in front of her tepee, wearing a traditional buckskin dress decorated with beads and shells.

When the first Europeans arrived, six main Native American groups lived in North Dakota. The Arikara, Mandan, and Hidatsa settled in and near the Missouri River valley. They built lodges and farmed. During the warmer months, they headed onto the plains to hunt game such as deer and bison. When the snows came, they often settled down in one place for the winter.

The Chippewa lived in the northeastern portion of the state, while the Yankton Sioux lived near the James and Cheyenne rivers. They were great bison hunters and became skilled riders when the horse was introduced to the region. The Lakota, or Teton Sioux, were North Dakota's most powerful Native American nation. The Lakota gained control of the southwestern part of the state and much of the plains beyond.

Early Settlers

North Dakota's official written history begins in 1738 when Frenchman Pierre Gaultier de Varennes, Sieur de la Vérendrye, and his sons briefly visited the area. They reached a group of Mandan villages near present-day Bismarck and wrote a series of letters about their experiences.

The land that would become North Dakota changed hands several times from the late 1600s to the early 1800s. The southwestern part of the state was claimed by France in 1682. Later France claimed lands in Canada, stretching from Hudson Bay to the northeastern corner of the state. In 1713, France gave this portion of land to Great Britain. Then in 1762, France gave Spain the lower section of its holdings. This included all of its land west of the Mississippi River. Spain then decided to give the land back to France in 1800. In 1803, the final change of ownership occurred. The United States bought 828,000 square miles (2,144,510 sq km) of land from France. The land included parts of present-day North Dakota and all or portions of fourteen other future states. This land deal was called the Louisiana Purchase.

Dogs were more than just pets for the often nomadic Mandan people. Before they acquired horses, the Mandan would pack up their belongings and hitch them to teams of dogs, which dragged the items across the plains to the group's next stopover.

President Thomas Jefferson was curious to know more about the land his government had just bought. So in 1803 he sent Meriwether Lewis and William Clark west to explore the land and to forge a trail to the Pacific Ocean. The two brave adventurers reached North Dakota in late October in 1804. They met with a council of Mandan and Hidatsa leaders and offered them presents from the US government. The gifts included a flag, a medal bearing the image of Jefferson, the coat of a uniform, and a hat with a feather. "But none seemed to give them more satisfaction," Lewis wrote, "than an iron corn mill which we gave to the Mandans."

MAKING A CHIPPEWA STICK-DICE GAME

Many Chippewa enjoyed playing a game that used stick-dice. These instructions will show you how to make the stick-dice and play a game.

WHAT YOU NEED

4 large tongue depressors (available at craft stores or pharmacies)
Black, red, yellow, and white tempera paint
Paintbrushes

TO MAKE THE STICK-DICE

The tongue depressors will be the sticks. Paint one side of each tongue depressor black. Set the sticks aside and let them dry. When the black paint is dry, paint small yellow and white designs over the black paint on each stick. You can paint Xs, dots, or short lines. Once the paint is dry, turn the sticks over. Paint a long, red squiggly line down the length of two of the sticks. Leave the other two sticks blank.

TO PLAY THE GAME

You need two players for this game. Each player takes a turn throwing the sticks down on a cloth or blanket. Players earn points for the way the sticks fall. The sticks represent snakes. The black sides are the snakes' backs. The other sides are the snakes' bellies. The two snakes with the red lines on their bellies are called the senior stick-dice. The other two snakes with unmarked bellies are the junior stick-dice. Points are determined by how all four sticks fall.

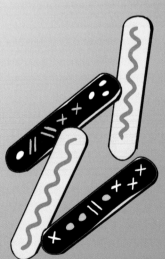

There are only four ways to score points:

All backs.. 4 points
All bellies .... 4 points
Both senior snakes belly up .... 2 points
Both junior snakes belly up.................... 1 point

You each continue to throw until a player earns five points. At that point an extra throw is called. The player with the lower score throws first. Then the player with five points throws. If the player with five points scores higher during the extra throw, then he or she wins the game. If the other player's extra-throw score is higher, then the player with the five points loses points according to the opponent's throw: all bellies or all backs, the five-point player loses four points. Any other winning throw, the five-point player loses two points.

Points won in the extra throw are not added to the regular game points of either player. If there are no points earned by either player in the extra throw, extra throws continue until points are earned. After the extra-throw points have been deducted from the five-point player, regular play continues. Using the points that each has left, the game proceeds until someone gets to five points again. At that point, another extra throw round is called. The final winner of the game is the player who reaches five points in regular play AND wins the extra-throw round.

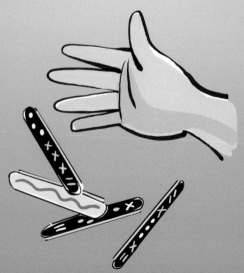

On the eastern bank of the Missouri River, near present-day Stanton, the explorers built Fort Mandan. They stayed there until April 1805 when it was time to push farther west. It was the most time they had spent in any one place while on their journey. Or, as Fort Mandan's tourist slogan puts it, "Lewis and Clark slept here (146 times)." The pair also passed through the state again in 1806 on their trip back to the East.

Lewis and Clark's journey was an important first step in settling the region. Slowly, over the next century, people from far-off places would make their way to North Dakota. In 1812, Scottish and Irish families from Canada built the state's first settlement at Pembina.

Most settlers first came to the area in search of furs. From the mid-1700s, the French and British had competed to control the fur trade with the Native Americans. Later the Spanish tried without success to get their share of the profits. After the Louisiana Purchase, control of the fur trade slowly tipped to the American side. By the mid-nineteenth century, fur companies had built trading

This George Catlin painting from 1832 shows the earthen lodges of a Hidatsa village along the Knife River. Native American life was dramatically disrupted when white settlers pushed westward onto the plains.

This painting by Karl Bodmer shows Fort Union, on the Missouri River. Trading posts were the shopping malls of their day, places where goods, services, and news were readily exchanged.

posts along the Mississippi River valley and driven out British trappers and traders. From 1828 to 1867, Fort Union Trading Post was the main fur-trading station in the upper Missouri River region. The success of trading in the region led to better transportation routes. More settlements also sprang up along the plains.

Indian Wars

The discovery of gold in California and Montana in the 1840s and 1850s brought even more traffic to the state. Pioneers heading west began to blaze their trails through traditional Native American lands. North Dakota's Native Americans were not pleased with the arrival of these newcomers. For years the fur trade had been good for both Native Americans and Europeans. The peace and calm were about to end, though. As more newcomers entered the region, the Native American way of life began to change. Gradually Native Americans lost control of lands that had been their home for centuries. They could no longer hunt or live on much of their land.

In this photograph from the late 1880s, a track gang lays part of the St. Paul, Minneapolis, & Manitoba Railway Company line, from Minot, North Dakota, to Montana.

Starvation, broken treaties, and the continued loss of land led to the Minnesota Uprising of 1862. Hundreds of Minnesota settlers were killed by Lakota Indians, who then fled into North Dakota. The government sent Generals Henry Hastings Sibley and Alfred Sully to capture the Native American rebels. In 1863, Sibley led 2,300 Minnesota infantrymen into the northern part of the territory. Sully led 2,000 soldiers north up the Mississippi River from Iowa. On September 3, 1863, the forces beat the native fighters at the Battle of Whitestone Hill. They then went on to destroy many other Native American camps in the area.

In 1864, in the Killdeer Mountains, Sully's troops attacked a large camp of Native Americans, driving them west into the badlands. Sully's men gave chase but soon became lost in the badland's twists and turns. Although the Native Americans escaped that assault, the attacks continued. Another major campaign was launched in 1865. The government's plan to push the Native Americans farther west was working. Though small skirmishes continued, North Dakota's Native Americans were mostly defeated. Peace finally arrived in 1881, when the great leader Sitting Bull surrendered. Afterward, many Native Americans were required to live on reservations.

Sitting Bull became chief of the Lakota people in 1868. He resisted the US takeover of Indian lands and was killed in 1890 when authorities feared he would join an uprising at the reservation where he lived.

Railroads, such as this one though the Dakota Territory, allowed settlers to travel great distances in a much shorter time than they could in wagons or on horseback.

"A Delightsome Land"

The Dakota Territory was created in 1861. It was named for the Lakota word meaning "friends" or "allies." It included all of present-day North and South Dakota and large parts of Wyoming and Montana. In 1863, the territory was opened to settlers who wanted to farm the land. Called homesteaders, they were offered free patches of land if they lived on it and worked it for a given number of years. The government expected several thousands, but only a small trickle of people flowed into the state. They came by wagon, steamboat, and stagecoach.

Many settlers thought that the region was too far from everything. Most pioneers headed to places that were not quite so remote or to places farther west. By the early 1870s, only about 30 families had officially registered their land claims. Territory officials needed to find a way to draw more people to the Dakota Territory.

In the 1870s and 1880s, the railroads and the government joined forces. They took out advertisements that promoted settlement in the Dakota Territory. The ads called the Dakotas "a delightsome land," where free—or cheap—land awaited them, "ready for the plow." The Northern Pacific Railroad started laying track across northern parts of the state in 1872. Slowly the population was starting to grow.

By the late 1870s, large farming operations were established in the state. Families and companies from the East set up huge wheat farms. The farms ranged from 3,000 to 65,000 acres (1,214–26,305 ha) and were mostly found in the Red River valley. They were so successful and earned such large profits, they were called bonanza farms. Ranching also became popular in the region. Cattle companies spread into the badlands. Future US president Theodore Roosevelt helped open up land for ranching along the Little Missouri River. By 1889, more than 2,000 miles (3,219 km) of railroad tracks crisscrossed the state. The region was finally prepared to join the Union. On November 2, 1889, North Dakota officially became a state.

When Theodore Roosevelt left North Dakota, he returned to his birthplace of New York City and ran for mayor. He lost the election, but became the president of the United States just a few years later, in 1901.

North Dakota's capital city is Bismarck. Originally called Edwinton, the city was renamed in 1873 for Otto von Bismarck, the leader of Germany.

By the 1890s the boom was over. Not as many people moved into the state. Wheat prices started to fall. Many of the large bonanza farms were divided into smaller properties. The state's residents continued to make money, but on a smaller scale. Still, North Dakota continued to grow. Coal mining was introduced to the region. Newcomers still came to claim the available land. Many arrived from faraway places, and the region slowly became a blend of cultures. Most of the state's new residents came from Norway, Germany, and Russia. Great numbers also arrived from Finland, Canada, Denmark, England, Ireland, Sweden, Hungary, Scotland, and Austria.

Life was often hard for these settlers trying to squeeze a living out of the land. To claim their land, residents had to build at least a one-room home on their property. However, wood was scarce on the mostly treeless northern plains. Some families ordered lumber and hauled it for miles (km) from the closest railroad station. Unfortunately, few could afford such a luxury. The settlers were forced to be creative. They looked to the land for an answer. Some scooped large holes out of the banks of streams. These homes were called dugouts. Most settlers chose to build with sod. This was the top layer of soil which was held firmly together by the roots of the grasses. Settlers cut great chunks of sod out of the prairie and shaped it into blocks. The blocks were stacked to form simple homes. Sod proved to be a good building material. It was inexpensive and fairly sturdy. Sometimes wind, rain, and small animals forced their way through the cracks and seams in these sod houses, though. Some German and Russian settlers began building homes made of bricks of sun-dried mud. Eventually, many pioneer families made their homes out of this material.

A Call for Change

Starting in the 1880s, North Dakota's farmers were faced with new challenges. Fighting drought and harsh weather was hard enough, but now the railroads added to their problems. Some North Dakotans felt that the railroad companies had too much control. The farmers needed the railroads to ship their products to markets in the East. However, the railroads often charged high prices for their services. Few farmers could afford these expenses. In 1884, a group of farmers formed the Dakota Farmers' Alliance (DFA). Within four years, the group had 28,000 members. Together they built grain elevators and warehouses to store their crops. They also started a group to buy coal and supplies. Combining

The peak of prairie ingenuity, the sod house made use of one of the few building materials the treeless plains offered.

their goods and money made it easier to ship and sell their goods. They also published a magazine called *Dakota Farmer*. The alliance slowly gained power and popularity. By 1892, the DFA had strong political power in the state legislature.

Groups such as the DFA were formed not just to fight the railroads. Other organizations worked together to fight political "bosses." These were powerful and wealthy business leaders who controlled much of the state. By the 1890s, "Boss" Alexander McKenzie had a tight grip on North Dakota politics. He bribed officials in order to create the state lottery. He controlled the selection of state senators in 1893. Concerned citizens wanted to end this imbalance of power and to lessen the bosses' control.

The University of North Dakota, in Grand Forks, is the largest university in the state. It was established in 1883, six years before North Dakota became a state.

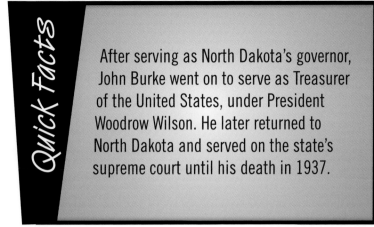

Change came in the first decade of the 1900s. A spirit of reform was slowly gripping the state. In 1907, Democratic governor John Burke took office and called for sweeping changes. He passed a series of laws aimed at railroad reform, child labor protection, worker's compensation, and food and drug purity. Students benefited from the reforms as well. Education improved as the state began training more qualified teachers. Soon one-room schoolhouses were established in places where no schools had existed before. More colleges opened their doors for the first time in the state.

From the late 1890s to the mid-1910s, North Dakota experienced another boom. Better farm machinery and more effective farming methods were two of the driving forces. About 25,000 new residents—still mostly Europeans—arrived during this period.

By the 1910s, the control of the political bosses had ended. Farmers continued to look for ways to make their lives easier. In 1915, they formed the Nonpartisan League. Within a year, 40,000 farmers had joined. The group believed the state should own grain-processing centers, shipping centers, and storage areas. It also called for banks that would grant farmers low-interest loans to be set up in agricultural areas.

Tough Times

In the 1920s hard times hit the state once again. Weather patterns changed, and a series of droughts gripped most of North Dakota. Dust storms raged in the western part of the state, which only added to the problems. Throughout the 1920s and 1930s there was little rain. Grasshoppers descended on the land, destroying crops. The price of grain also dropped. To make matters worse, diseases such as stem rust infected much of the state's wheat crop.

In 1929, the United States was faced with the Great Depression. Across the country people lost their jobs and could not find ways to support their families. Farmers began to suffer, too. Because of the weak economy, few people could afford to buy farm produce. In North Dakota many families lost their homes. Banks foreclosed on, or took away, their homesteads. Before long, the banks began to fail and were forced to close. By 1933, more than half of North Dakota's banks had failed. Of the 898 that were found in the state in 1920, only 343 remained.

The Great Depression was a terrible time for many North Dakotans. With crops damaged by drought, grasshoppers, and disease, there was little food or water to feed livestock and horses, and many animals died of starvation.

Relief came in the form of a series of programs run by the US government. The Works Progress Administration (WPA) hired people to build highways, wells and irrigations systems, sewage-treatment plants, schools, and recreation sites across the state. From 1934 to 1941, the Civilian Conservation Corps (CCC) worked near Medora. Workers there cleared and restored the 128-acre-(52 ha) Chateau de Mores State Historic Site and the De Mores Memorial Park. Projects such as these provided much-needed jobs for North Dakotans. Historian Elwyn B. Robinson wrote that during the 1930s, relief was "the biggest business in the state."

World War II also helped the state's economy recover. North Dakota supplied food and other goods to the troops. In the early 1940s, the state's fields and farms were producing more grain than ever before. Soon, though, surpluses, or too much grain, developed. As a result, the prices of these crops started to fall again. It was another shift the state was forced to face. In the last half of the twentieth century, fewer farms dotted the North Dakota landscape. Machines replaced workers in the fields. People started moving to the cities and larger towns in search of jobs.

Into the Future

In the last half of the twentieth century, North Dakota continued to grow and change. Officials needed to create new jobs and industries and, at the same time, protect the state's environment and resources. In 1968, the Garrison Diversion Project began. It included a system of canals that channeled water from the Missouri River to the state's farmland. The system was also designed to supply water to several North Dakota cities and towns. During the 1970s, though, progress on the project slowed. Citizens worried that the project might harm the state's environment. The Canadian government protested the fact that polluted waters might drain into Canada's rivers. In 1986 Congress voted to alter the plan and lessen the possibility of future damage.

Agriculture remains one of the most important industries in North Dakota. Crop production remained high in the 1980s and 1990s. However, state officials

The floods of 2011 once again forced many people in the state to evacuate, or leave, their homes.

have begun to worry about relying so heavily on farming. The state has learned from the past that natural disasters, such as droughts and floods, and smaller crop profits can quickly create hard times.

Tough times are nothing new to North Dakotans. The state has continued to face new challenges. In 1997, after a winter of record snowfall, the Red River overflowed, causing the worst flood in state history. The overflow spread through many riverfront cities. In some places, such as Grand Forks, the water reached more than 50 feet (15 m) high. Almost 90 percent of the residents of Grand Forks were forced to leave their homes. More than 70 percent of the city's buildings were damaged by the water. North Dakotans in the area rolled up their sleeves and went to work, piling sandbags to stop the flow. Many people opened their homes to families forced out by the rising waters.

Riverfront cities have learned from these floods. New safety measures are in place. Some riverfront buildings have been raised to higher levels, and ponds have been created to hold extra water that overflows. When major floods hit the area again in 2009 and 2011, residents were ready. Nature and hard times have not always been kind to the state, but North Dakotans continue to prove they are up for the challenges of life in the Peace Garden State.

Important Dates

★ **1600s** Several Native American groups have been living in the state for centuries.

★ **1682** France lays claim to the land that includes North Dakota.

★ **1738** French explorer Sieur de la Vérendrye is the first European to enter parts of present-day North Dakota.

★ **1781** A trading post is built by settlers near the Souris River.

★ **1803** The United States buys land from France that includes most of present-day North Dakota.

★ **1804–1806** Explorers Meriwether Lewis and William Clark reach North Dakota on their way to the Pacific Ocean. They pass through again on their way back east.

★ **1812** Pembina becomes the state's first official community, founded by Scottish and Irish settlers.

★ **1861** The Dakota Territory is created by the US Congress.

★ **1863** The Dakota Territory is opened to settlers.

★ **1870** The Sioux and Chippewa give up most of their land in eastern North Dakota.

★ **1872** The first railway line is laid across North Dakota.

★ **1889** North Dakota officially becomes a state.

★ **1930s** Severe droughts add to the hardships of the Great Depression.

★ **1947** Theodore Roosevelt National Park opens.

★ **1951** Oil is discovered near Tioga.

★ **1988** Drought strikes the state for the first time since the Great Depression.

★ **1997** Flooding in the Red River valley damages cities and towns and forces people from their homes.

★ **2008** Oil from the Bakken Formation leads to an oil boom and gives the state the lowest unemployment rate in the country.

★ **2011** The Red River valley is again hit by damaging floods.

The People

North Dakota prides itself on its close-knit communities. The isolation of the prairie tends to bring people together. Because so few people are spread across so much land, many residents learn to help one another. As the state has moved into the twenty-first century, North Dakotans stand united. The state continues to face new issues, such as the loss of farms and a continued shift from country living to more urban areas. The challenge is nothing new to North Dakotans, though. They have survived droughts, floods, and blizzards. As one resident puts it, "To live here, you've got to be tough."

Heritage

According to the US Census in 2010, about 90 percent of the people in North Dakota trace their roots to Europe. Some North Dakotans are descendants of Europeans who came hundreds of years ago. Others have lived in North Dakota for only a few years. Today, immigrants from European countries continue to move to the state.

> ## In Their Own Words
>
> *I was born in a very small town in North Dakota, a town of only about 350 people. I lived there until I was 13. It was a marvelous advantage to grow up in a small town where you knew everybody.*
>
> —Warren Christopher, former US secretary of state

People of Native American heritage have always been and continue to be an important part of North Dakota.

A troupe performs traditional dances at the Norsk Hostfest in Minot, a celebration of North Dakota's Scandinavian heritage.

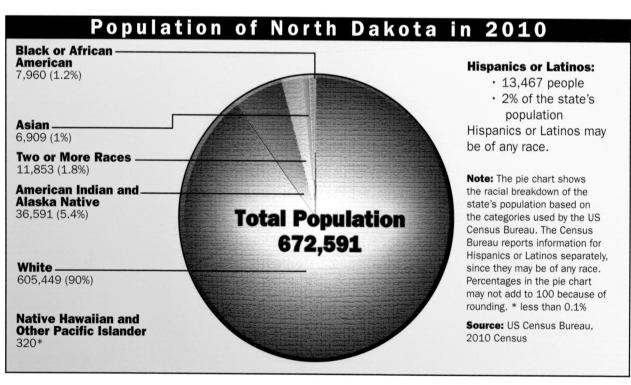

Population of North Dakota in 2010

Black or African American
7,960 (1.2%)

Asian
6,909 (1%)

Two or More Races
11,853 (1.8%)

American Indian and Alaska Native
36,591 (5.4%)

White
605,449 (90%)

Native Hawaiian and Other Pacific Islander
320*

Total Population 672,591

Hispanics or Latinos:
· 13,467 people
· 2% of the state's population
Hispanics or Latinos may be of any race.

Note: The pie chart shows the racial breakdown of the state's population based on the categories used by the US Census Bureau. The Census Bureau reports information for Hispanics or Latinos separately, since they may be of any race. Percentages in the pie chart may not add to 100 because of rounding. * less than 0.1%

Source: US Census Bureau, 2010 Census

A children's choir pays tribute to the rich and varied musical heritage of the plains.

Many North Dakotans trace their roots to Scandinavian countries. In the late 1800s, more than a million people left Norway and headed for the United States. Many settled in North Dakota and on the northern plains. People also arrived from Sweden, Denmark, and Finland, blending in with the new society forming in the early days of the state. Today there are several festivals honoring this northern European heritage. People come from across the state to celebrate traditional arts, food, and music. Colorful Scandinavian costumes are often on display at these gatherings.

Other ethnicities are represented in North Dakota, but in smaller numbers. About 1.5 percent of the population is African American. Many are active in the state's communities and government. The same can be said for the Hispanic people in North Dakota. They make up about 2 percent of the population. Some Hispanics come to North Dakota to work on farms. Others move to the cities to work in the thriving businesses. Asians and Asian Americans also account for about 1 percent of the population. Many live and work in North Dakota's cities. Others move to the more rural areas of the state.

Though the majority of the state's residents are of European heritage, people of all ethnicities play an important role in North Dakota's rich and vibrant culture.

For the most part, the state has responded positively to its immigrant populations. The government has set up information centers and hotlines that help newcomers solve legal issues, obtain citizenship, and understand state laws. City officials have appointed officers who work specifically with immigrant communities.

No matter where they come from, many of these newcomers from different backgrounds continue to honor their native cultures while also embracing American traditions and ways of life. Religious services and cultural celebrations can be seen in different parts of the state. The North Dakota government has also approved more money to develop programs and activities that celebrate the state's blend of cultures.

Native North Dakota

The first people to populate the region that included North Dakota were Native Americans. Today, Native Americans make up about 5.5 percent of the state's population. North Dakota takes its Native American tradition seriously and celebrates it with pride. The Mandan, Hidatsa, Arikara, Yanktonai, Sisseton, Wahpeton, and Hunkpapa (divisions of the larger group known as the Lakota, or Sioux) along with the Pembina Chippewa and Cree all add to the state's rich cultural heritage.

North Dakota's Native Americans live across the state in cities and in small towns. Many also live on the state's five major reservations. Cattle ranching and farming are vital parts of the economy of the reservations. Tribe-owned businesses, such as casinos and lodges, are also important. The money earned from these businesses goes toward maintaining the reservations, as well as providing health care and education for Native Americans. Most of the

Keith Bear, a Native American storyteller and musician, plays the flute in a traditional earthen lodge at the Knife River Indian Villages National Historic Site.

reservations also have their own community colleges and technical schools.

Like many other North Dakota communities, the state's Native Americans are also exploring new ways of earning a living. At Fort Totten, for example, the Spirit Lake Nation owns the Sioux Manufacturing Corp, which produces a type of armor called Kevlar, which is worn by soldiers in the US Army.

North Dakota is also the site of a push to protect and restore Native American languages. Long before European settlers arrived with their own languages, a wealth of native languages was spoken on the plains. Leaders now seek to preserve that diversity. Linguists, or people who study languages, have joined forces with educators in North and South Dakota to help preserve the Lakota language. This is the language of the nation that once dominated vast stretches of the Great Plains. About half of America's 100,000 Lakota currently live on reservations on the western plains. Experts fear that very soon fewer people will be able to speak their native language. In the next twenty to fifty years, there is the threat the language will completely die out.

In the late 1800s and early 1900s, the government discouraged the use of Lakota. In government-run boarding schools, Native American students caught speaking their native language were punished. This pattern mostly ended by the 1930s, but by then the damage had been done. The Lakota language was used less frequently. Not until the Lakota gained control of their reservation schools in the 1970s were attempts made to revive the language. However, there was little money available to train teachers or to set up organized ways to teach younger generations the language.

Under a group called the Lakota Language Consortium, educators set up a plan to rewrite the curriculums of the school districts that teach large populations of Lakota children. Doug Parks, assistant director of the American Indian Institute, pointed out that most school curriculums are written with white, middle-class students in mind. "There is just no way that Lakota students who live in isolated conditions on a reservation can relate to that," he said.

Dancers prepare to perform during a traditional gathering of the Spirit Lake Sioux Tribe at the Fort Totten Reservation.

In 2008 and 2011, the Lakota Language Consortium published dictionaries in the Lakota language. Also in 2011, the group translated 20 episodes of a children's cartoon into Lakota and the episodes were shown on public television in North and South Dakota. This was the first time an animated cartoon had been shown entirely in a Native American language.

Tied to the Land

Farming has been a long and proud tradition in the Peace Garden State. The experiences of the people who worked the state's farms are a central part of North Dakota's history. However, many North Dakotans whose families once worked the land have today found better opportunities and an easier life in the state's more urban areas. North Dakota's farmers have faced new and greater struggles in recent years. More and more machinery is used on the state's farms. That means fewer workers are needed. Low crop prices have spelled disaster for many farmers. Some have been forced to sell their land.

Famous North Dakotans

Warren Christopher: Former Secretary of State

Born in Scranton in 1925, Warren Christopher first made a name for himself as a skilled lawyer. As deputy secretary of state from 1977 to 1981, he helped secure the release of 52 American hostages held in Iran. On January 20, 1993, Christopher was sworn in as the sixty-third secretary of state.

Chuck Klosterman: Writer

Chuck Klosterman was born in Minnesota but grew up on a farm in Wyndmere. He graduated from the University of North Dakota and began his writing career as a journalist in Fargo. He has written for many popular magazines and has published several books, a few of which take place in North Dakota.

Phil Jackson: Athlete and Coach

Born in 1945, Jackson attended high school in Williston and went on to play professional basketball for the New York Knicks. After ending his career as a basketball player, Jackson went on to become one of the most successful coaches in NBA history. He coached the Chicago Bulls to six championships in the 1990s, and then went on to lead the Los Angeles Lakers to five championships in 2000–2002 and 2009–2010.

Kellan Lutz: Movie Star

Model and actor Kellan Lutz was born in Dickinson in 1985. He grew up in a large family, with six brothers and one sister. He has acted in many television shows and films, including *The Twilight Saga* series.

Peggy Lee: Singer and Actress

Peggy Lee was born in Jamestown in 1920. She first displayed her talents singing on many of North Dakota's radio stations. Eventually she made her way to California where she became one of the leading entertainers of her generation. In addition to singing, Lee was also a songwriter and an actress. She had more than 40 hit singles and was nominated for an Academy Award.

Roger Maris: Baseball Player

Maris was born in 1934 in Hibbing, Minnesota, but grew up in Fargo. Maris played many sports and was offered a football scholarship to the University of Oklahoma. He decided instead to enter professional baseball. As a New York Yankee, he became the American League's most valuable player in 1960. In 1961 he set the record for the most home runs in a season with 61—a record that stood for almost forty years.

Just a few years ago, North Dakota's population was dropping and state officials struggled to find ways to keep young people in the state. Then, in 2008, workers began extracting oil from the Bakken Formation, a rock formation beneath land in North Dakota, Montana, and parts of Canada. The oil boom has meant many changes for the state, both good and bad. In many areas, the population has grown very quickly as workers from across the country come

North Dakota has always been known as an agricultural state. In recent years, though, farming and ranching have been on the decline.

to North Dakota for jobs. The state government has made a lot of money, and North Dakota now has the lowest unemployment rate in the United States. However, the oil boom has also put a strain on sewage systems, roads, and water supplies.

Oil Boom

The oil boom has changed North Dakota in other ways, too. The workers coming to drill oil are mostly male. This has created a population in some towns with many more males than females. The arrival of so many people has also caused housing prices to rise, which many state residents are not able to afford.

The residents of Arnegard ride their horses down Main Street during a Fourth of July parade. Many North Dakotans take pride in the close-knit communities found in the state's many small towns.

These bison cross the Little Missouri River, in Theodore Roosevelt National Park. Keeping areas such as this park clean and free of pollution is vital to the safety of many plants and animals.

Oil drilling has affected the state's environmental areas, too. Theodore Roosevelt National Park, for example, has seen increases in traffic and pollution. Increased noise in the park can also have negative consequences for animals. It can affect the way they communicate with each other and find mates, which can lead to lower levels of reproduction. Fewer babies is a major problems for animal species that are already threatened or endangered.

Another effect of the drilling is flaring, or the burning off of natural gas. While flaring causes less pollution than some other methods, it still releases about 60 types of pollutants into the air.

It is clear that the state's current oil boom has its pros and cons. Over the next few decades, as more oil is drilled, the state will likely face many challenges as it tries to balance job growth and a strong economy with adequate infrastructure and environmental concerns. North Dakotans are up to the challenge, though. Like early settlers, today's residents work to find creative solutions to difficult problems.

Some experts think North Dakota could have as many as 48,000 oil wells in the next few decades.

★ Wild West Jamboree

This festival kicks off in West Fargo in June. Shootouts, stagecoach rides, country music, and cowboy poetry all take you back to the early days of the American West. The highlight of the jamboree is the Great West stage show performed daily.

★ German Folk Festival

People from all around gather in Fargo each July and celebrate the area's German heritage with music, costumes, and food. In addition to booths with arts and crafts, special performances are often scheduled. One year, a 45-piece youth band from Germany performed.

★ North Dakota State Fair

The North Dakota State Fair, held each July in Minot, features a long list of things to see and do. Booths, exhibits, rodeo events, car shows, a carnival, and live entertainment all compete for the attention of fairgoers. The State Fair Center shows the best the state has to offer—from food to flowers, vegetables, and prize animals.

★ Killdeer Mountain Roundup Rodeo

Held every year for almost 90 years, this is the state's oldest rodeo. In July, people gather in Killdeer to experience daring displays of bull riding, roping, and riding bucking broncos.

★ Central North Dakota Steam Threshers Reunion

This is one of New Rockford's biggest annual events. It is held the third weekend of September and boasts a variety of antique farm machinery, tractor rides, dancing, and craft shows.

★ Norsk Hostfest

This October event is the largest Scandanavian festival in North America, attracting tens of thousands each year. Held in Minot, the fair's highlights include live musical performances, crafts, and food.

★ Great Tomato Festival

This fun event, held in August, features a silent auction, live music, and a menu full of tomato-based treats. The money raised from the event benefits community organizations in Minot, such as the public library, art museums, and the symphony orchestra.

★ Windfest

Held in Kulm, this August festival celebrates North Dakota's wind farms. The event features a water carnival, mechanical bull, lawn mower races, and a fun run.

How the Government Works

North Dakotans want a bright future for their state. They look to their leaders to make strong choices and decisions that will benefit all. The state's politicians must deal with many important concerns. They are still debating the best way to face the future. No one person can decide the path the state should take. Instead the right course is decided through debate and compromise. The process is open to everyone. New laws or policies are often suggested by the state's voters. Many citizens have good ideas about how their state could be better run. In North Dakota, it is important that many voices are heard. After all, new laws and policies affect the lives of everyone.

North Dakotans do not have to be politicians working at the capitol building in Bismarck to serve their state. There is plenty to be done to improve life in their own communities. The state's citizens serve their local governments in countless ways. They often act as lawmakers and managers and make decisions that influence local lives. The state currently has nearly 400 towns and cities. Each of these local units chooses how they want their community to be run. The daily affairs of the city may be overseen by a mayor, a council, a manager, or a board of commissioners. These leaders make sure that roads are safe and citizens have

The state capitol building in Bismarck is the tallest structure in the area. On the long sweep of lawn in front of the capitol stands a statue called *The Pioneer Family,* a tribute to the state's first white settlers.

access to government-run services and programs.

The county is another important level of state government. North Dakota is divided into 53 counties. Each county is run by a board of commissioners. The boards have three to five members who serve terms of four years. Board members are responsible for most aspects of county business. They must ensure that all of the county's communities are equally served. Financial planners, sheriffs, school superintendents, and state attorneys are just some of the people who play a vital role in the life of North Dakota's counties.

State officials have the hard job of running the state as a whole. They collect and spend the state's funds on a variety of programs and projects. They also serve in departments or on boards that deal with a specific aspect of life in the state. Native American affairs, agriculture, tourism, wildlife, and the arts are just some of the areas on which various officials focus. Some state leaders make sure North Dakota's citizens and highways are safe, while others work on bringing new companies and more businesses to the state. There are many jobs to be done in a state in which citizens have a wide range of needs and concerns.

From Bill to Law

The process by which a bill becomes a law often involves many steps. When a citizen or legislator has an idea for a law, it must first be proposed in written form. A group called the Legislative Management then gives the bill an official number and has it printed so that every legislator can read what is being proposed. The bill's title is then read by the secretary of the senate or the chief clerk of the house of representatives, depending on which house is introducing the bill. This is known as the first reading.

Branches of Government

EXECUTIVE ★ ★ ★ ★ ★ ★ ★ ★

The governor heads the executive branch. He or she is elected to a four-year term. This official helps create the state budget and makes sure the state's business runs smoothly. Other elected officials help the governor. They include the lieutenant governor, the secretary of state, the state treasurer, and the attorney general.

LEGISLATIVE ★ ★ ★ ★ ★ ★ ★ ★

The state's legislative assembly is divided into two parts. The senate has 47 members. The house of representatives is made up of 94 elected officials. Together the members help to make the laws that all North Dakotans must follow. Many of these legislators, or lawmakers, also serve on committees. They focus on issues that are important to the state such as agriculture and education.

JUDICIAL ★ ★ ★ ★ ★ ★ ★ ★

North Dakota's Supreme Court is made up of five justices, or judges. They serve for ten years. They decide important cases or issues that were not cleared up by the state's lower courts. Most of North Dakota's trials take place in district courts.

Next, the bill is open for discussion and debate. It is then referred, or sent, to what is called a standing committee. The state has several standing committees. Each group focuses on a particular topic or issue. A bill about fishing licenses, for example, would be sent to the Natural Resources Committee. The assigned

The North Dakota legislature meets in the nineteen-story capitol building in Bismarck. It is often referred to as the "skyscraper on the prairie."

committee then holds a public hearing. The state's citizens are welcome to attend these important meetings and express their views. This is when certain points of the bill are debated. After the committee has looked into all parts of the bill, it reports back to the other members in the house. They either pass, do not pass, amend—or change—the bill, or refer it to another committee that will look into it in more depth.

The chamber of the legislature that first proposed the bill then votes on it. If the members are in favor of the bill, it moves on to the other half of the state's legislature, either the senate or the house of representatives. Once there, the bill goes through a similar process. A committee examines and discusses it. Often it makes new changes or suggestions. If that happens, the bill has to be approved by both parts of the legislature again. If each agrees, the bill is then signed by the leader of the senate and the house of representatives. It is then sent to the governor.

Contacting Lawmakers

★ ★ ★ ★ ★ ★ ★ ★ ★ ★ ★ ★

If you are interested in contacting North Dakota's state legislators, go to

http://www.legis.nd.gov/

You can search for legislators and their contact information by name, zip code, or district.

The governor can either approve the bill or veto, or reject, it. If he or she vetoes it, the bill is sent back to the legislature. Two-thirds of both the senate and the house of representatives must vote in favor of the bill if it is to become a law. Once a bill is approved, it is sent to the secretary of state and made official. In North Dakota, most new laws take effect on August 1 of each year.

North Dakota's house of representatives meets in this chamber of the capitol building.

Making a Living

North Dakota is farm country. Agriculture helped to build the state and make it strong. Though the farm industry is starting to decline, it continues to be a major source of the state's income. Residents and government officials have long supported laws and programs that would help the state's farmers. Powerful groups such as the Nonpartisan League forever changed the way the state does business. In the 1910s and 1920s they pushed a series of reforms, such as lower taxes, that would ease the farmer's way of life. To this day, in the minds of many North Dakotans, farmers and ranchers come first.

In 1957, the Economic Development Commission was set up. It was created to attract businesses to the state. The idea caught on, and now more than 80 communities have similar groups. As time goes on, the state has also looked for other ways of earning money. While farming will continue to be important to the state's economy, leaders are searching for new ways, such as oil production, to keep the state thriving in the twenty-first century.

A ranch dog gets a rare moment of rest after a long day of herding cattle. Ranching and farming are very important to the state's economy.

North Dakota's Industries and Workers (June 2013)

Industry	Number of People Working in That Industry	Percentage of Labor Force Working in That Industry
Mining and Logging	29,500	6.6%
Construction	32,000	7.2%
Manufacturing	25,600	5.7%
Trade, Transportation, and Utilities	98,900	22.3%
Information	6,900	1.5%
Financial Activities	22,900	5.2%
Professional & Business Services	34,600	7.8%
Education & Health Services	58,300	13.1%
Leisure & Hospitality	38,000	8.6%
Other Services	15,500	3.5%
Government	80,800	18.2%
Totals	**467,674**	**99.7%**

Notes: Figures above do not include people in the armed forces.
"Professionals" includes people such as doctors and lawyers.

Source: U.S. Bureau of Labor Statistics

North Dakota farmers only began growing large amounts of dry beans in the 1960s. Today they produce about 38 percent of the country's beans, more than any other state!

Agriculture

North Dakota's economy cannot be examined without taking a look at agriculture. Much of the state's wealth is locked in its soil. Almost 90 percent of the state's land is devoted to farming and ranching. The state is a top producer of barley, durum spring wheat, all types of dry edible beans, dry peas, oats, sunflowers, and flaxseed. It ranks second in the production of navy beans and pinto beans. North Dakota is one of four states that produces the most potatoes, sugar beets, and honey.

Cows are key to the state's farm economy. A well-fed cow can produce nearly 200,000 glasses of milk in its lifetime.

RECIPE FOR HONEY AND PEANUT BUTTER COOKIES

North Dakota produces more than 34 million pounds (15.4 million kg) of honey each year. The honey is sold throughout the state and across the country. Here is a recipe for making about two dozen tasty cookies using this sweet product.

WHAT YOU NEED

1 cup honey
1/4 cup softened butter or margarine
3/4 cup peanut butter
1 1/2 cups all-purpose flour
1/2 teaspoon baking soda
1/2 teaspoon salt
1 egg
1 teaspoon vanilla extract

Combine the honey and butter in a mixing bowl. Add the peanut butter, egg, and vanilla extract. Stir this mixture until it is well blended. Slowly add the flour, baking soda, and salt, mixing well as you pour.

Grease a large baking sheet and evenly space the drops of cookie dough. Each cookie should have about one tablespoon of dough. Using a fork, gently flatten each drop of dough.

Have an adult help you use the oven. Set the temperature to 350°F (177°C). Bake the cookies for about twelve minutes. Have an adult remove the cookie sheet from the oven because it will be hot. Gently place the cookies on a cooling rack. Once they are cool, grab a glass of milk and enjoy!

Barley is grown mostly in eastern North Dakota, while the bright, bobbing faces of sunflowers blanket the drift prairie region. Corn is plentiful along the southern plains. The corn helps feed the state's hogs. Grass thrives across the state as well. It is cut, dried, and gathered into bales or piles. The hay is then used mostly to feed North Dakota's large herds of cattle.

Livestock is another major part of the state's economy. The vast grasslands of central and western North Dakota offer the ideal place for cattle to roam and graze. The state's cows are not raised only for their meat, though. Dairy farms dot the southern plains. Hogs are raised mostly on smaller farms in the south and southeast. Some North Dakota ranches also raise sheep.

Like other midwestern farm economies, the state has witnessed a gradual decline in farming through the years. Today there are about 31,600 farms and ranches in North Dakota. That is about half the number that existed in the 1950s.

Row upon row of shimmering wheat is harvested on this farm south of Binford, in Griggs County.

This welder is hard at work at a tractor factory in Fargo.

This decrease in the number of farms has not delivered a major blow to North Dakota's economy, though. While there are fewer farms overall, farm size has increased over the years. Improved machinery means smaller operations can successfully farm more land.

Mining

North Dakota land is rich in many minerals. When oil was discovered near Tioga in 1951, it became North Dakota's most valuable mined product. Slowly the oil industry developed in the state, and by 1970 there were oil wells in fourteen western North Dakota counties. Today, North Dakota is the second largest oil-producing state, and workers are drilling more and more oil every day. During May of 2013, 800,000 barrels of oil were produced, which was a new monthly record.

North Dakota also has major deposits of lignite coal. Lignite coal, also called brown coal, is used as a fuel source. Officials estimate that 400 to 600 billion tons (363 billion to 544 billion t) of lignite coal lie beneath western North Dakota. The southwest is rich in various types of clay used for pottery and brick-making. Sand and gravel are important products found across the entire state. They are used mainly for building roads.

Manufacturing

With so many crops being grown in the Peace Garden State, it makes sense that food processing is also an important industry. Cities such as Fargo, Grand Forks, Minot, and Bismarck rely on the state's agricultural products for a major part of their annual income. Factories and business centers in these cities process grain, meat, and dairy products.

The state's many varieties of wheat are turned into pasta and bread. Potatoes are peeled, sliced, and made into enough French fries to supply many fast-food restaurants for a year. Milk is placed in containers and shipped to stores across the area or turned into delicious cheeses. The meat produced in the state becomes steaks and sausage. North Dakota's workers help to keep their state and the nation well fed.

North Dakota factories also produce farm equipment and supplies. Farm-related items are not the only products made. The state's workers also make cabinets and furniture, computer software, construction equipment, and airplane parts.

Retail and Services

The various jobs that make up North Dakota's service industries account for a large part of the state's annual income. These businesses are mostly located in or near the state's urban centers. Grocery stores, restaurants, gas stations, and hardware stores all add their share to North Dakota's earnings. Real estate is also an important part of the economy. This is mostly because large amounts of land need to be bought and sold for the state's farms and ranches.

Grand Forks, Bismarck, and Fargo have large medical centers that employ thousands of people. Law firms, hotels, and shops that repair cars and farm equipment also contribute to the economy.

Transportation is very important to North Dakota. People need to be able to travel around the large state. The state's valuable farm and mineral products must also be shipped great distances to urban centers. Pipelines funnel oil and natural gas, while trucks and trains haul the state's crops and coal. Without these

Products & Resources

Sunflowers

North Dakota grows more sunflowers than any other state. The state produces about 50 percent of the country's crop. The flowers are sold to nurseries and florists across the state and around the country. The seeds are sold in the United States and in Europe as well.

Oil

Since 2008, oil has become a major industry in the state, bringing in many new workers and tax dollars and making North Dakota the second-largest oil producing state in the country. Today there are almost 9,000 oil wells in the state, though there many be thousands more in the coming decades.

Honey

North Dakota is the nation's leading honey producer. North Dakota bees make almost 35 million pounds (15.8 million kg) of honey each year. The pure honey is often sold around the country. It is also combined with other foods in the state's food processing plants.

Farm Machinery

Farms are important to the economy, so it is not surprising that making and selling farm equipment is big business in North Dakota. The state has many factories that manufacture farm machinery. Some large plants are based in Fargo and Bismarck, while smaller operations can be found in Wahpeton, Minot, and Pembina.

Tourism

Tourism is North Dakota's third-leading source of income, adding nearly $5 billion to the state's economy each year. People come to see the badlands, the International Peace Garden, or to enjoy the wide, open spaces. Some people visit the state to see the world's largest bison monument, nicknamed Dakota Thunder. It is located at Frontier Village, in Jamestown, and is 26 feet (8 m) high, 46 feet (14 m) long, and weighs 60 tons (54 t).

Wheat

North Dakota is one of the country's top wheat-producing states, often trading off for the top spot with Kansas. For many years, countries around the world have imported different types of wheat from North Dakota. These types of wheat include hard red spring and durum.

Delicate clouds trail across the sky, reflected on the surface of wetlands in Grand Forks County. North Dakotans have strong ties to the land, which is the source of much of their inspiration and pride.

important transportation providers, the state would be unable to cash in on its agricultural and mineral wealth.

The first years of the twenty-first century have brought many changes to North Dakota. From a declining population and devastating floods to a record-breaking oil boom, a growing population, and a budget surplus, the state has seen many highs and lows.

Today, North Dakotans remain dedicated to their state and ready to grow. They still honor the traditions of the past and the ways of life that have guided their state steadily through the years. They also keep their eyes fixed on the future. Making success out of hard times, standing united and proud, North Dakotans know there are few challenges they cannot overcome.

State Flag & Seal

The state flag is dark blue with the United States coat of arms in the center. A banner beneath reads "North Dakota." The flag was adopted in 1911.

In the center of the seal, a Native American on horseback hunts a bison. Below him is a bow and arrow. These symbols stand for the state's proud native heritage. The bundle of wheat at the base of the tree, the plow, and the blacksmith's anvil (a tool used in making objects out of iron) all stand for the agriculture that is so important to the state. The state motto, "Liberty and Union Now and Forever One and Inseparable," wraps around the top of the seal. The seal was adopted in 1889.

North Dakota State Map

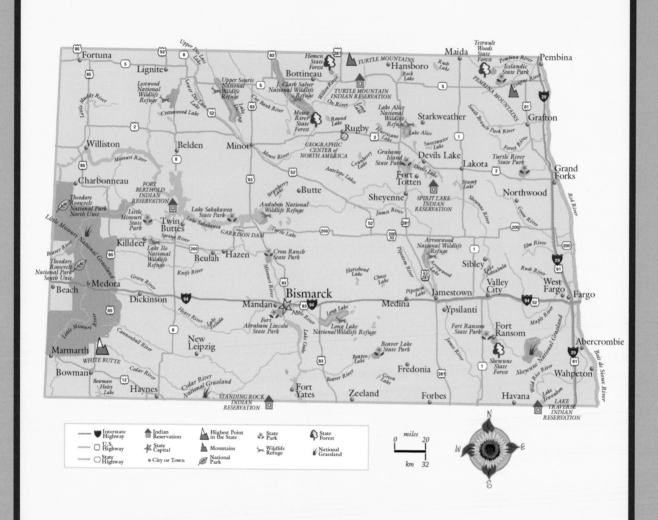

State Song

North Dakota Hymn

words and music by Arthur John Fynn

North Da - ko - ta, ___ North Da - ko - ta, ___ With thy prair - ies wide and free, All thy sons and daugh - ters love thee, Fair - est state from sea to sea; North Da - ko - ta, ___ North Da - ko - ta, ___ Here we pledge our - selves to thee. North Da - ko - ta, ___ North Da - ko - ta, ___ Here we pledge our - selves to thee.

MORE ABOUT NORTH DAKOTA ★ ★ ★

BOOKS

Fitzpatrick, Brad. *Theodore Roosevelt*. Conservation Heroes. New York: Chelsea House Publications, 2011.

Silverman, Robin Landew. *North Dakota*. From Sea to Shining Sea. Danbury, CT: Children's Press, 2009.

Stanley, George Edward. *Sitting Bull: Great Sioux Hero*. Sterling Biographies. New York: Sterling Publishers, 2011.

WEBSITES

North Dakota Parks and Recreation
http://www.parkrec.nd.gov/

North Dakota Tourism:
http://www.ndtourism.com

Official Portal for North Dakota State Government
http://www.nd.gov

Doug Sanders is the author of several titles in the It's My State! series. In writing this book, he drove across North Dakota, talking to the state's friendly residents along the way. His favorite place in the Peace Garden State is Theodore Roosevelt National Park, where he enjoyed hiking through the badlands.